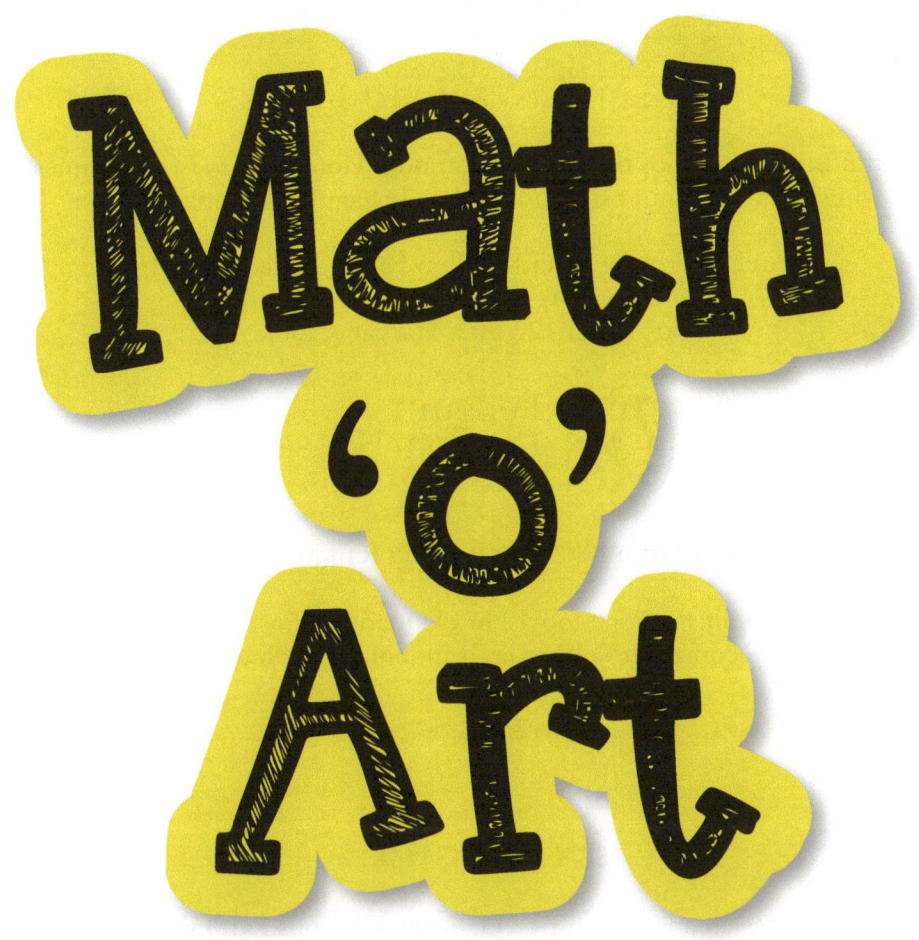

PUFFIN BOOKS

An imprint of Penguin Random House

PUFFIN BOOKS

USA | Canada | UK | Ireland | Australia
New Zealand | India | South Africa | China | Singapore

Puffin Books is part of the Penguin Random House group of companies
whose addresses can be found at global.penguinrandomhouse.com

Published by Penguin Random House India Pvt. Ltd
4th Floor, Capital Tower 1, MG Road,
Gurugram 122 002, Haryana, India

Penguin
Random House
India

First published in Puffin Books by Penguin Random House India 2018

Text, design and illustrations copyright © Quadrum Solutions Pvt. Ltd 2018
Series copyright © Penguin Random House India 2018

ISBN 9780143444817

Design and layout by Quadrum Solutions Pvt. Ltd

Printed at Repro India Limited

www.penguin.co.in

Dear Moms and Dads,

In the twenty-first century, logic skills have become an intrinsic part of the skills required for children to grow into confident adults. To be ready to absorb more complex mathematical concepts later in life, maths readiness has assumed greater importance than ever before. That is why it has become ever so important to prep children while they are young and eager to learn.

The **Fun with Maths** series seeks to do just that—let children loose on the joy of applying logic and building mathematical skills as they go.

We created these books for children to explore the wonders of mathematics. Here's a peek into what they will learn (without even knowing they have learnt it):

1 Mathematical operations such as addition, subtraction, division and multiplication

3 Patterns, symmetry and geometry

2 Logical reasoning and spatial awareness

4 Application of mathematics in everyday life

It's been great creating this series with my highly charged Quadrum team: maths experts Krupa Shah and Madhavi Nathan, who spent hours crafting each page; Himani, who designed every page into a visual treat; Dinesh, who provided creative guidance; Kushal, who painstakingly laid out every number and sign; Bishnupriya and Ruby, who read and re-read every word; and Kunjli, who was the conscience of the entire series. And, of course, the Puffin team, Sohini and Mriga, who added value at every step. When you have a great team, you're bound to have a great book.

Thank you, guys!

Sonia Mehta

PS: We'd love your feedback, so do write in to us at

funlearningbooks@quadrumltd.com

Hello Kids

Maths mixed up with art? Really! Whoever thought that was possible! Just imagine how nice it would be if all our maths was an art project. We could have loads of fun, while getting all the practice!

So if you love art, here's a book full of amazing activities that will let you enjoy being creative, while building your maths skills. There is

 **1** Colouring    **2** Drawing   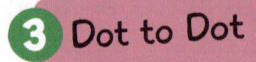 **3** Dot to Dot   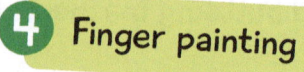 **4** Finger painting   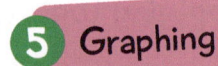 **5** Graphing

. . . and a whole lot more.

You will get to do some addition, subtraction, multiplication; you'll get to practice your logical and spatial skills; and you'll even dabble in time, patterns, geometry . . . and a whole load of maths concepts. By the end of it, you will have some amazing art to show your parents and friends. So get your glue, crayons, colour pencils or paints ready, and let's get started!

Math-o-Bot Challenge

Watch out for the Math-o-Bot challenge pages. They will get your creative juices flowing, and let you experience maths in a completely different way!

So it's time to bring out the maths genius and artist in you.

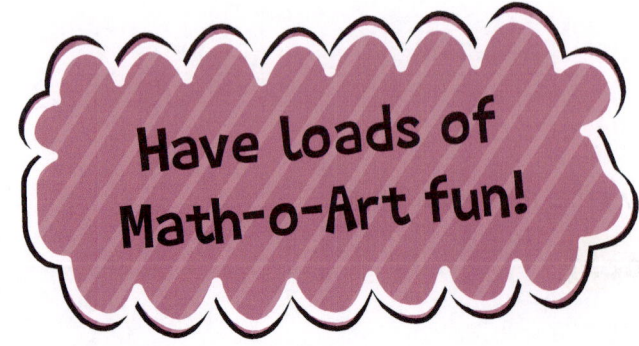

Have loads of Math-o-Art fun!

Flower Power

It is your mother's birthday and she loves a bunch of flowers! Draw the same number of petals on the stems as the answers for the clues below.

Stem 2: Your shoe size

Stem 3: The number of the month you were born in

Stem 4: Your age

Stem 1: The number of people in your family including you

Stem 5: The class you study in

Place Value House

Look at the minis and rods used in the picture below and write the answers in the space provided. Colour all minis in red and rods in blue.

A mini is equal to 1; a rod is equal to 10.

Flat

Rod

Mini

There are _____ rods + _____ minis = _____

Create It

Here's the number 294.

If we expand 294, we get _____ hundreds + _____ tens + _____ units.

Now create an image of your choice using the flats, rods and minis you've got. Colour it to make it beautiful.

Math-It

A flat is a square made with 10 rods.

Expanded Dots

Here are numbers written in the standard form. Make dots with your fingers and paint on the abacus to show the number.

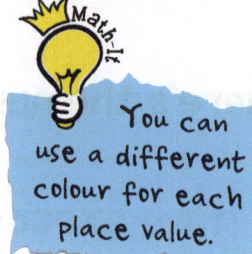

You can use a different colour for each place value.

H T U

45

H T U

124

H T U

207

H T U

360

Window Fun

The buildings below have many windows. Use the >, < or = sign to compare the number of windows in each building. Also, colour the building with the most windows green and the one with the least windows purple.

It's Raining!

Design your picture-perfect umbrella for those rainy days.
Solve the sums below to create a beautiful one!

Colour red if answer is 1 or 2   Colour blue if answer is 7 or 8
Colour yellow if answer is 3 or 4   Colour purple if answer is 9 or 0
Colour green if answer is 5 or 6

8 - 8   7 - 6

9 - 1   8 - 5

5 - 0   2 + 3

9 - 5   5 + 3

1 + 1   7 + 2

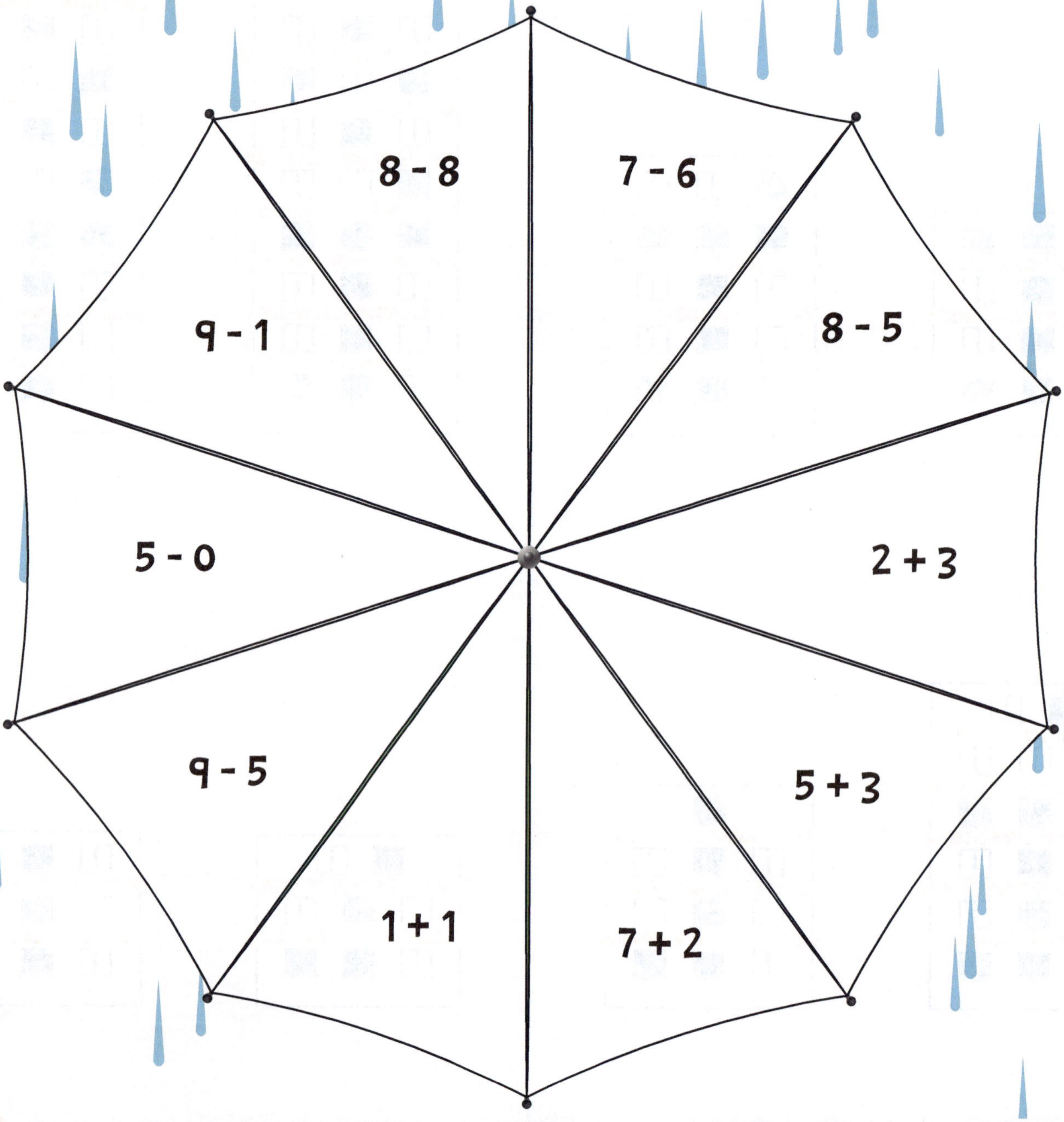

Sunshine

Add the number 31 to the number in each sun ray to get the answer. Colour the rays with an odd answer yellow and the rays with an even answer orange.

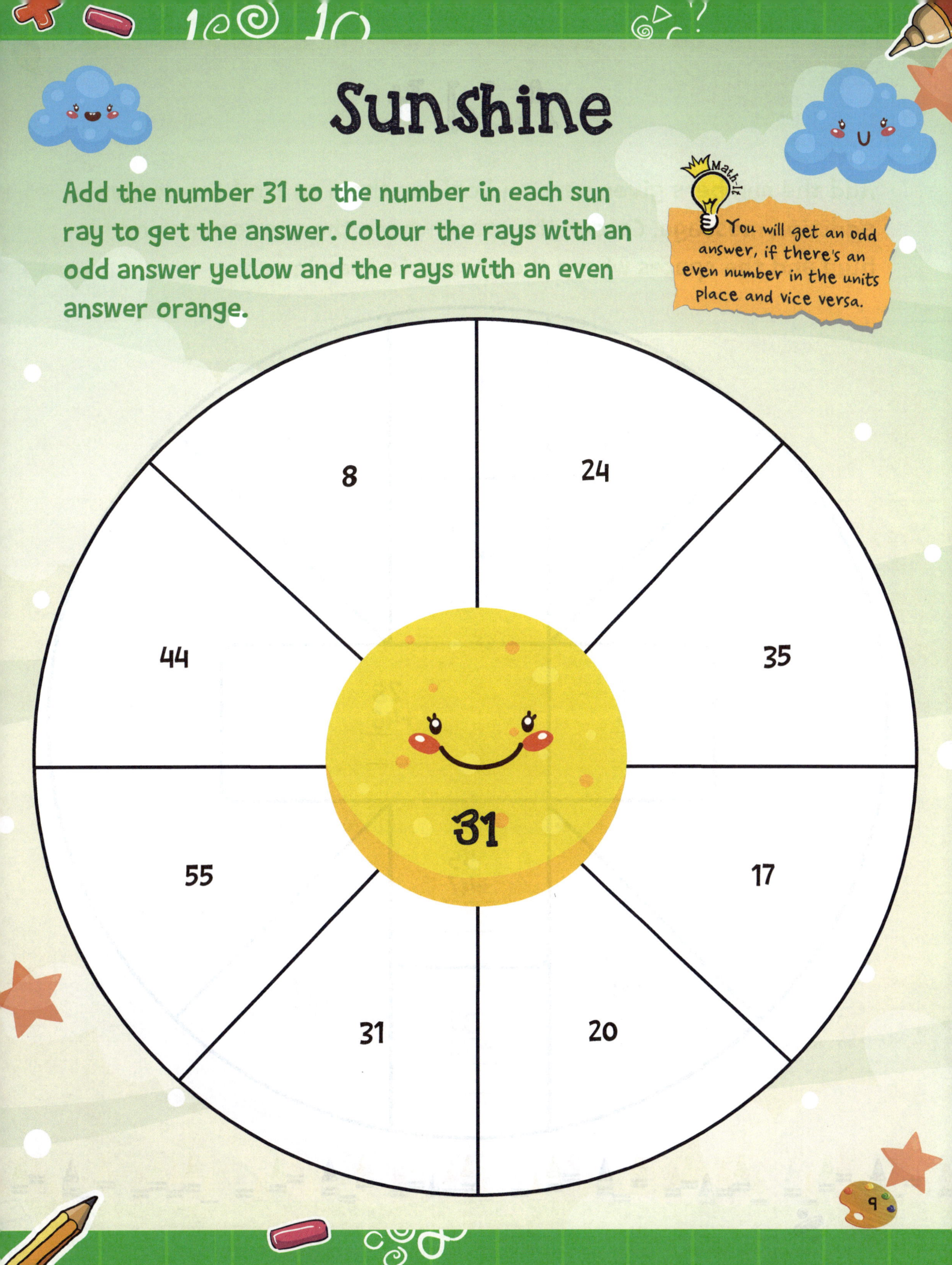

8

24

44

35

55

17

31

20

31

9

Add It

Add the numbers given here and colour them to find the hidden addition message. Colour the space where the answers are odd in blue and the spaces where the answer is even in red.

83
+38
____

71
+10
____

46
+49
____

37
+35
____

23
+48
____

18
+ 8
____

28
+46
____

39
+28
____

55
+47
____

23
+18
____

35
+30
____

41
+26
____

Subtract and Join

Solve the subtraction sums and then join the dots. Your answers must be in increasing order from 1 to 17. Colour the completed picture.

19-10   21-6

12-4   24-14   29-15   19-3

37-26   17-4

20-13   25-8

18-6

12-6   8-4   5-4

10-5

18-15   9-7

Sharpen Up

Subtract the numbers given here and colour to find the hidden image. If the answer is 5 or less, colour the space red.

Math-It
You must always subtract a smaller number from a greater number.

57
-31
___

66
-20
___

27
-22
___

76
-25
___

58
- 3
___

57
-54
___

87
-37
___

44
-44
___

89
-13
___

8
-4
___

28
-12
___

45
-31
___

4

Math-o-Bot's Challenge

Look at the pattern and continue it. It is a 2 (right), 3 (up), 4 (left), 5 (down) pattern.

Math-It

You don't have to continue the numbering, just the pattern. Use the same number pattern.

4

3

5

2
Starting Point

Blooming Butterfly

Solve the sums around the butterfly. Then colour using the code that matches the answer.

72 = Red   23 = Yellow   31 = Blue   13 = Orange   15 = Brown

95 – 23

35 – 12

62 – 47

87 – 15

68 – 45

50 – 19

61 – 48

52 – 37

67 – 36

32 – 19

Some sums need borrowing.

14

4

Candy Calculations

Solve the sums around the candy. Then colour using the code that matches the answer.

26 = Red
58 = Pink
80 = Blue
12 = Light green

45 = Orange
30 = Purple
72 = Dark green
34 = Yellow

9 + 17

26 + 46
90 - 60
22 + 23
64 - 30
23 - 11
35 + 45
70 - 12

12 + 14

Math-it

Be careful of the signs.

Coloured Arrays

Look at the numbers and create rectangles around them using the mentioned numbers. Count the squares inside to get the answer for the multiplication array. Then colour the rectangles in colours of your choice. One has been done for you.

3 x 4 = 12

4 x 5 = 20

3 x 3 = 9

6 x 4 = 24

5 x 7 = 35

8 x 3 = 24

6 x 5 = 30

7 x 2 = 14

Re-Re-Repeat

Join the numbers in skip counts of 3 to find the hidden image. Then colour it to make it look beautiful. Start at the red dot.

Remember to follow the correct order.

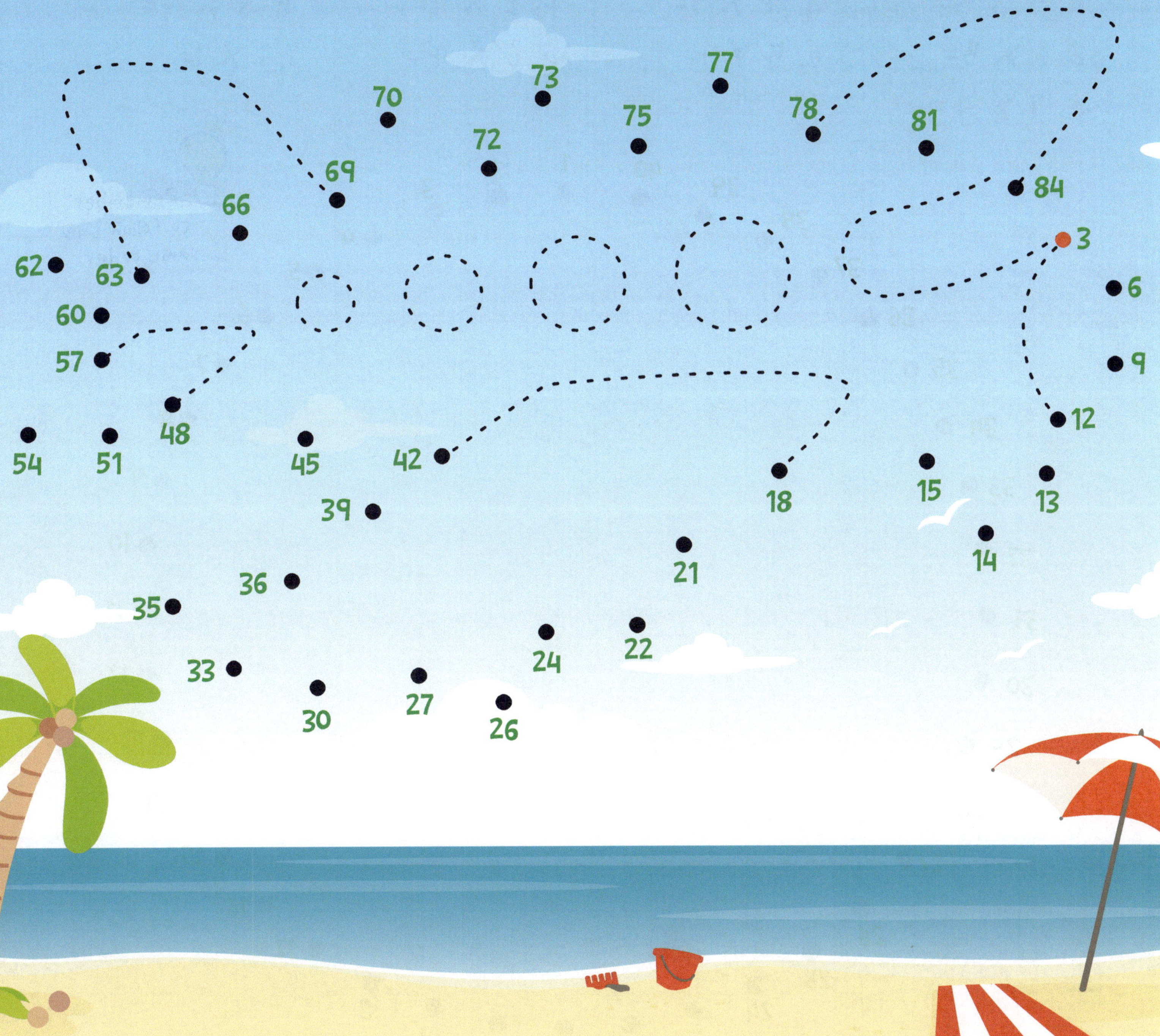

77
73
70
78
75
72
81
69
84
66
3
62 63
6
60
57
9
48
12
54 51
45 42
18
15
13
39
14
21
36
35
24 22
33
30 27 26

Circle Art

Solve the sums below. Mark them on the circle and join the numbers with straight lines to create a beautiful design. Start with 1. Follow the sums in the correct order.

a. 3 ✗ 3=

b. 6 ✗ 3=

c. 7 ✗ 4=

d. 4 ✗ 9=

e. 5 ✗ 1=

f. 2 ✗ 7=

g. 6 ✗ 4=

h. 8 ✗ 4=

i. 1 ✗ 1=

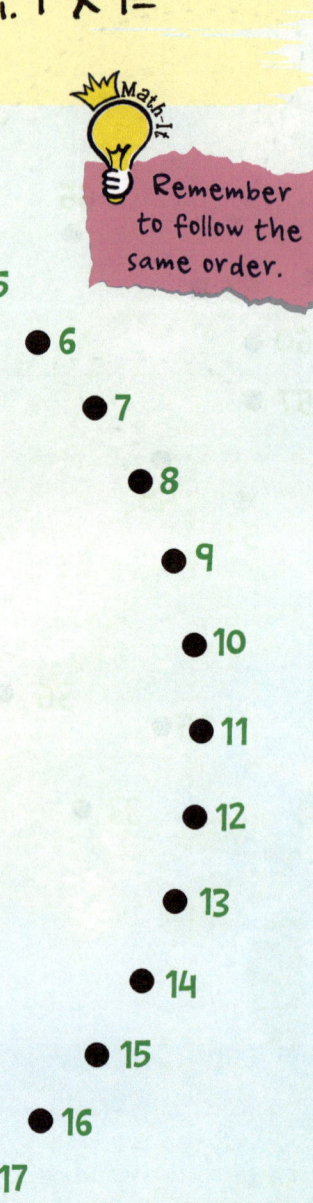

Remember to follow the same order.

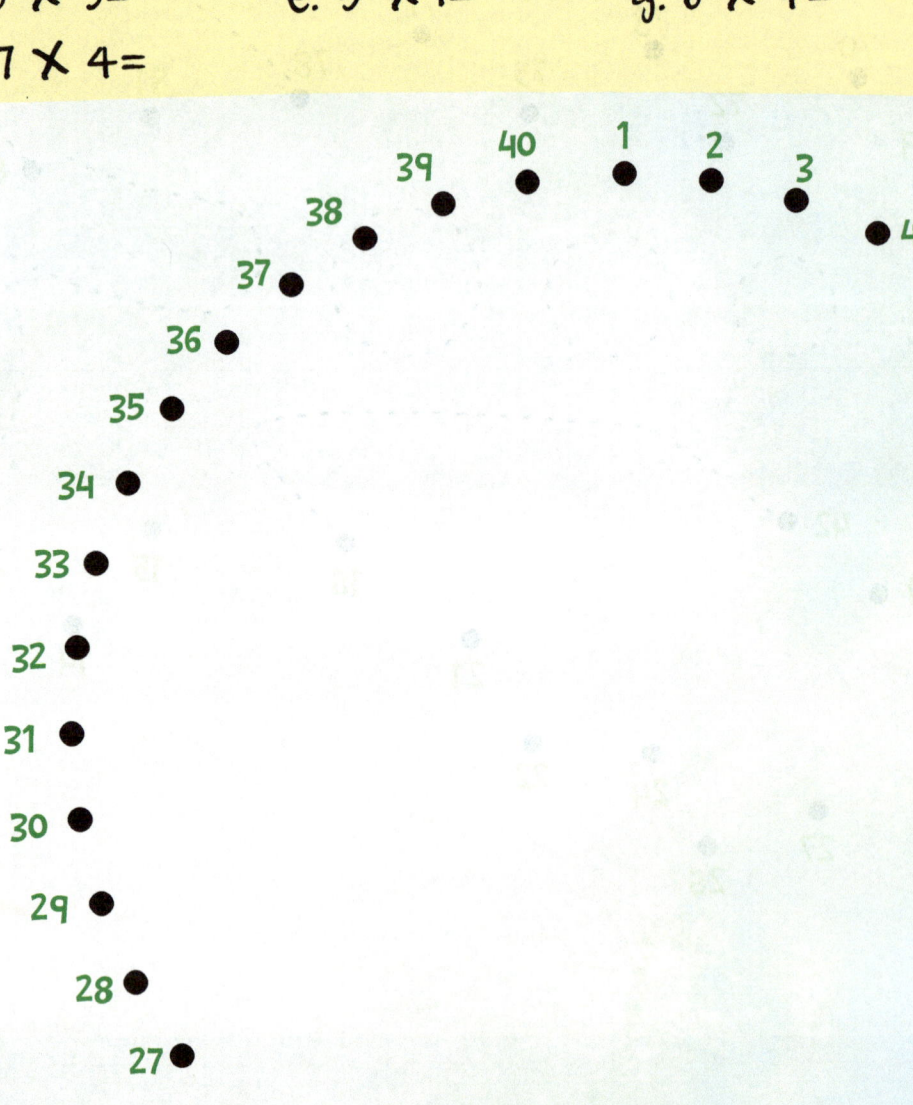

Floors and Windows

Add windows to the buildings below. The total number on windows and the floors in each building has been mentioned. Draw and colour the windows equally to find the number of windows on each floor.

1 12 windows and 4 floors
_____ windows on each floor

2 15 windows and 5 floors
_____ windows on each floor

3 16 windows and 4 floors
_____ windows on each floor

4 20 windows and 5 floors
_____ windows on each floor

5 25 windows and 5 floors
_____ windows on each floor

1   2   3   4   5

Gumballs

Given below are some division statements. Solve them and colour the image using the colour code that matches the answer.

10 ÷ 5 = ● (yellow)

0 ÷ 12 = ● (dark blue)

18 ÷ 2 = ● (orange-red)

12 ÷ 4 = ● (pink)

6 ÷ 6 = ● (light green)

24 ÷ 3 = ● (orange)

30 ÷ 6 = ● (green)

18 ÷ 3 = ● (light blue)

40 ÷ 4 = ● (grey)

16 ÷ 4 = ● (purple)

7 ÷ 1 = ● (brown)

House Rules

Each house has three numbers. Write the two possible multiplication and two possible division statements using the three numbers.

Multiplication and division are opposites.

House 1: 12 3 4

☐ × ☐ = ☐

☐ × ☐ = ☐

☐ ÷ ☐ = ☐

☐ ÷ ☐ = ☐

House 2: 2 8 16

☐ × ☐ = ☐

☐ × ☐ = ☐

☐ ÷ ☐ = ☐

☐ ÷ ☐ = ☐

House 3: 5 4 20

☐ × ☐ = ☐

☐ × ☐ = ☐

☐ ÷ ☐ = ☐

☐ ÷ ☐ = ☐

House 4: 6 4 24

☐ × ☐ = ☐

☐ × ☐ = ☐

☐ ÷ ☐ = ☐

☐ ÷ ☐ = ☐

Circle Time

Draw circles in the space below, then paint the overlapping shapes to create fun shapes and designs. Use different-sized circles.

Shaper

Draw the following shapes in the space below, then paint the overlapping shapes to create fun shapes and designs. Use different-sized shapes.

3 squares, 5 triangles, 2 circles, 1 rectangle, 2 diamonds

 # 15 Dots

Fill in the grids with dots made with your finger and paints. Each row, column and diagonal must add up to 15 dots.

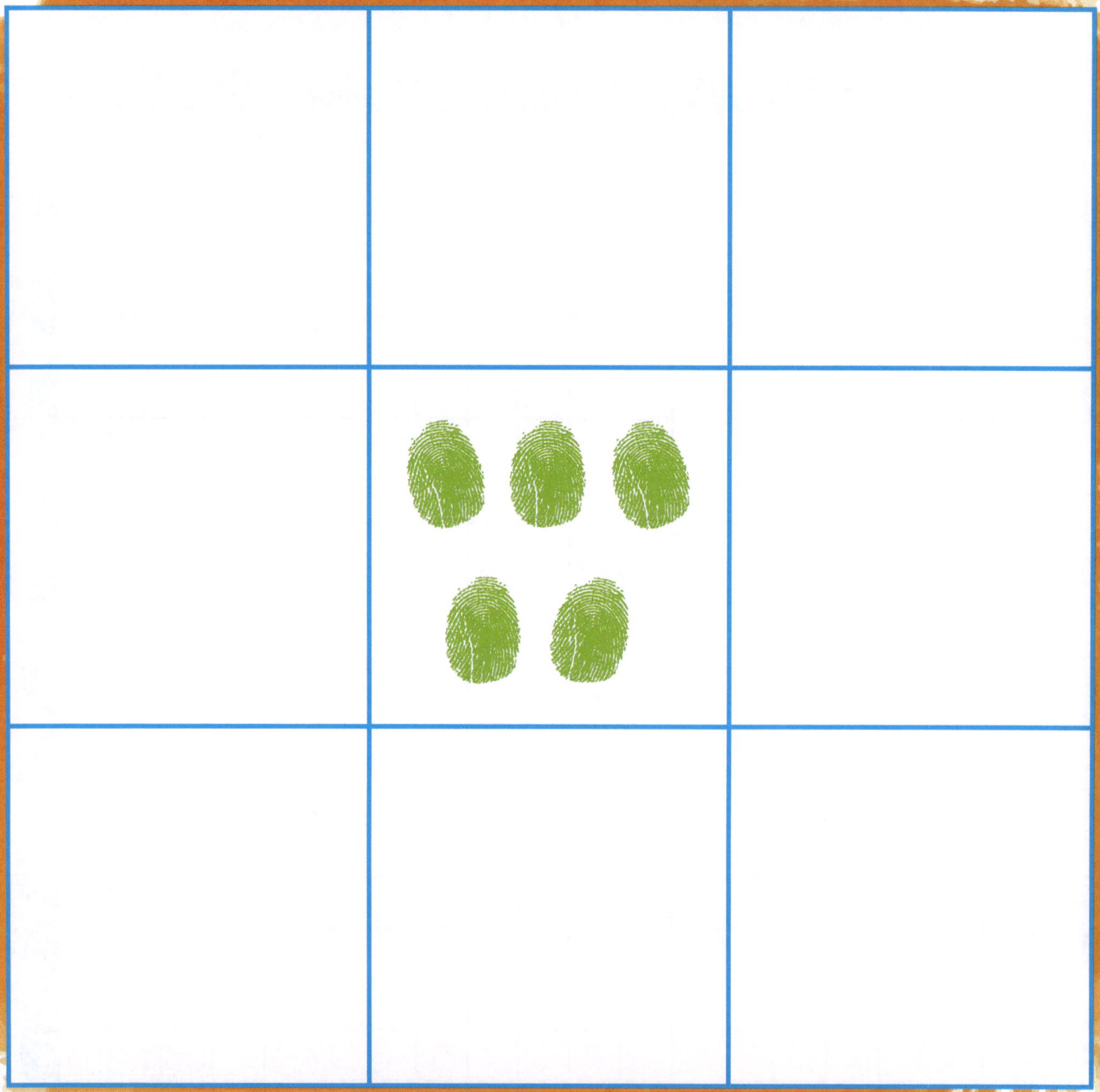

Starry Night

It's simple to make a 5-point star. Now let's make stars with more points. Start with a dot of your choice and join every third dot. Then colour it.

Gift Boxes

Let's make some 3D gift boxes for Christmas. First draw a square or a rectangle. Then draw slanting lines from the 3 corners and join them with straight lines. Now decorate the gifts.

Funny Faces

Add details to the faces using different shapes. Then colour the faces.

Tessellations

Complete the following tessellations and colour them.

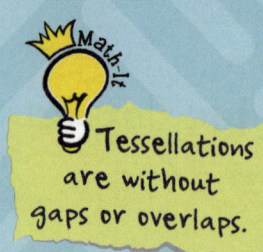

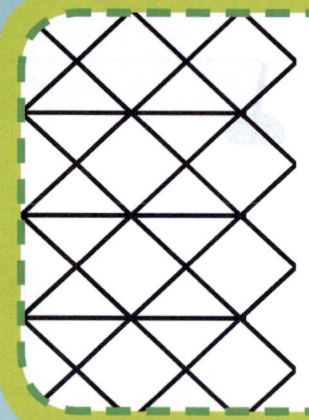

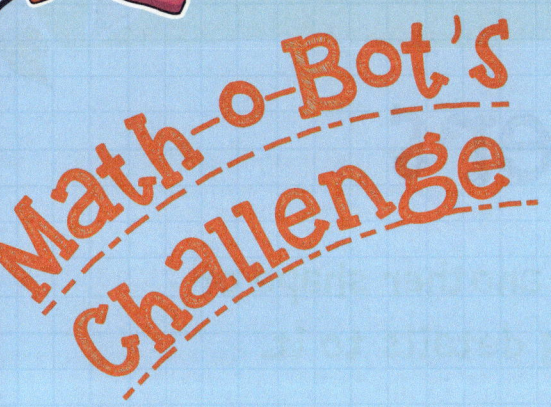

Math-o-Bot's Challenge

Tessellations are so much fun. Let's learn to create your own unique shapes and trace them on a paper to create your own tessellations.

You can add more details to make a more complex tessellation.

Square

Cut one side

Tape to opposite side

Tessellating shape is formed

transformers

You have to transform the first shape into another shape or object by changing it bit by bit or by adding details to it.

Painted Caterpillars

The caterpillars here have different patterns. Identify the pattern and then complete it using your fingers and paints.

Symmetrical Objects

Here are some objects you see around you.
Colour the symmetrical objects.

Math-It
Shapes that are not symmetrical are called asymmetrical.

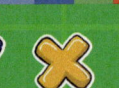

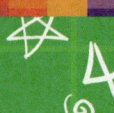

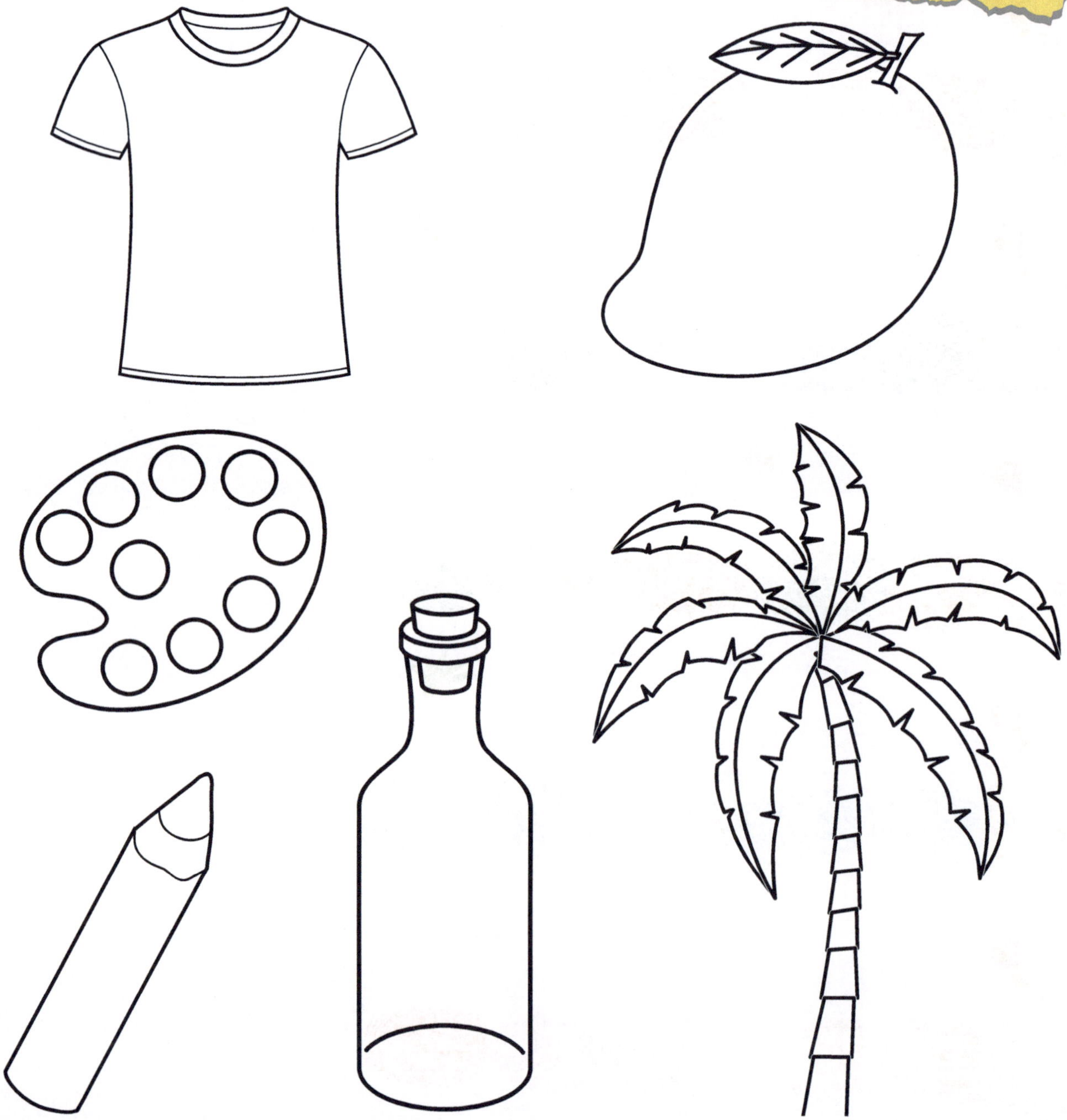

Symmetrical Penguin

Draw the other part of the penguin and then colour the picture.

Use the grid to help you.

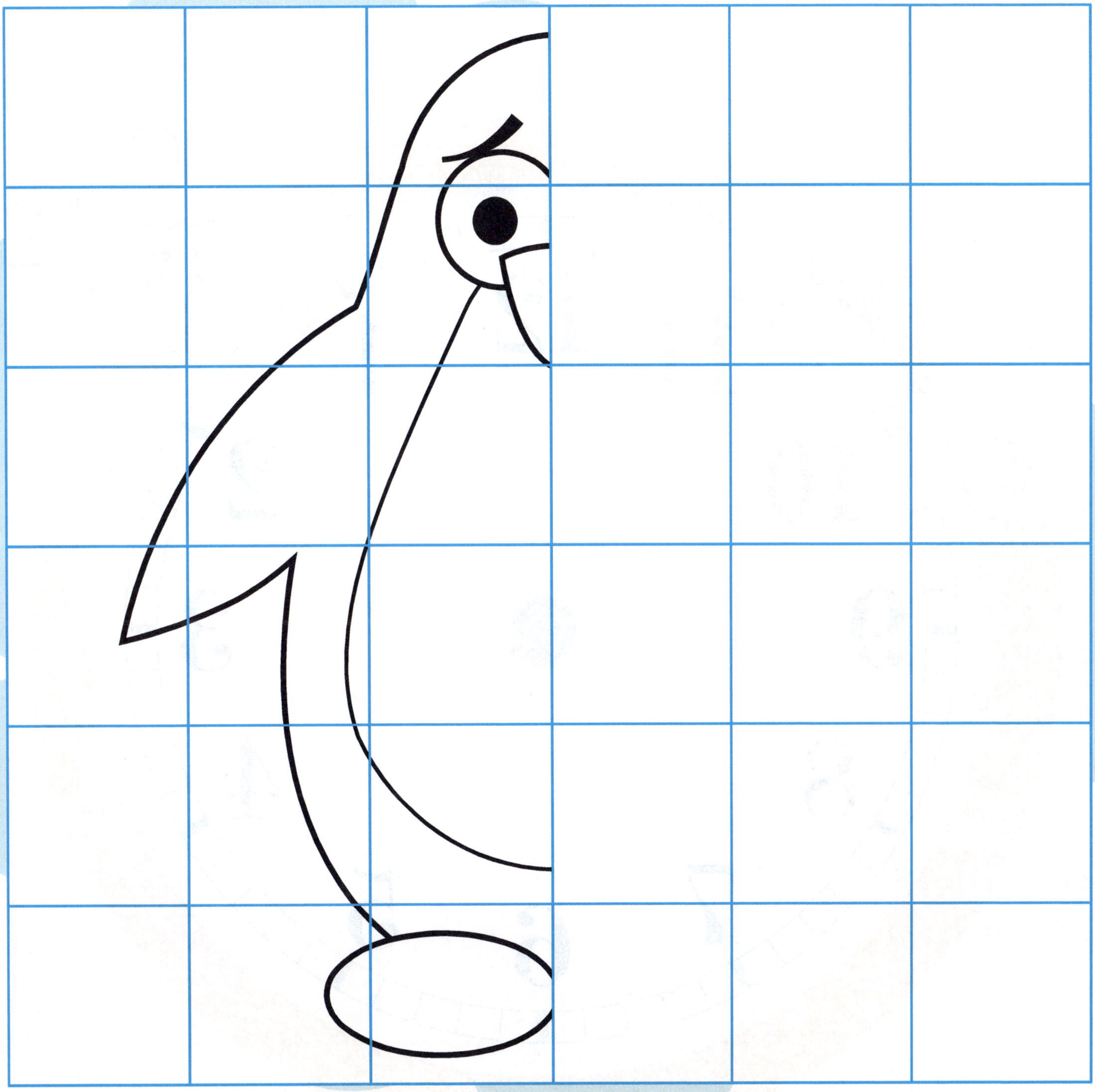

Karen's Clock

Here is Karen's schedule for the day. Look at the colour mentioned against each activity and use the same colour on the clock.

Karen gets ready from 7 to 8 🟢   Karen goes to school from 8 to 2 🔴

Karen sleeps from 3 to 4 🟡   Karen plays from 5 to 6 🔵

Math-It
You have to mark both am and pm schedules together on the same clock.

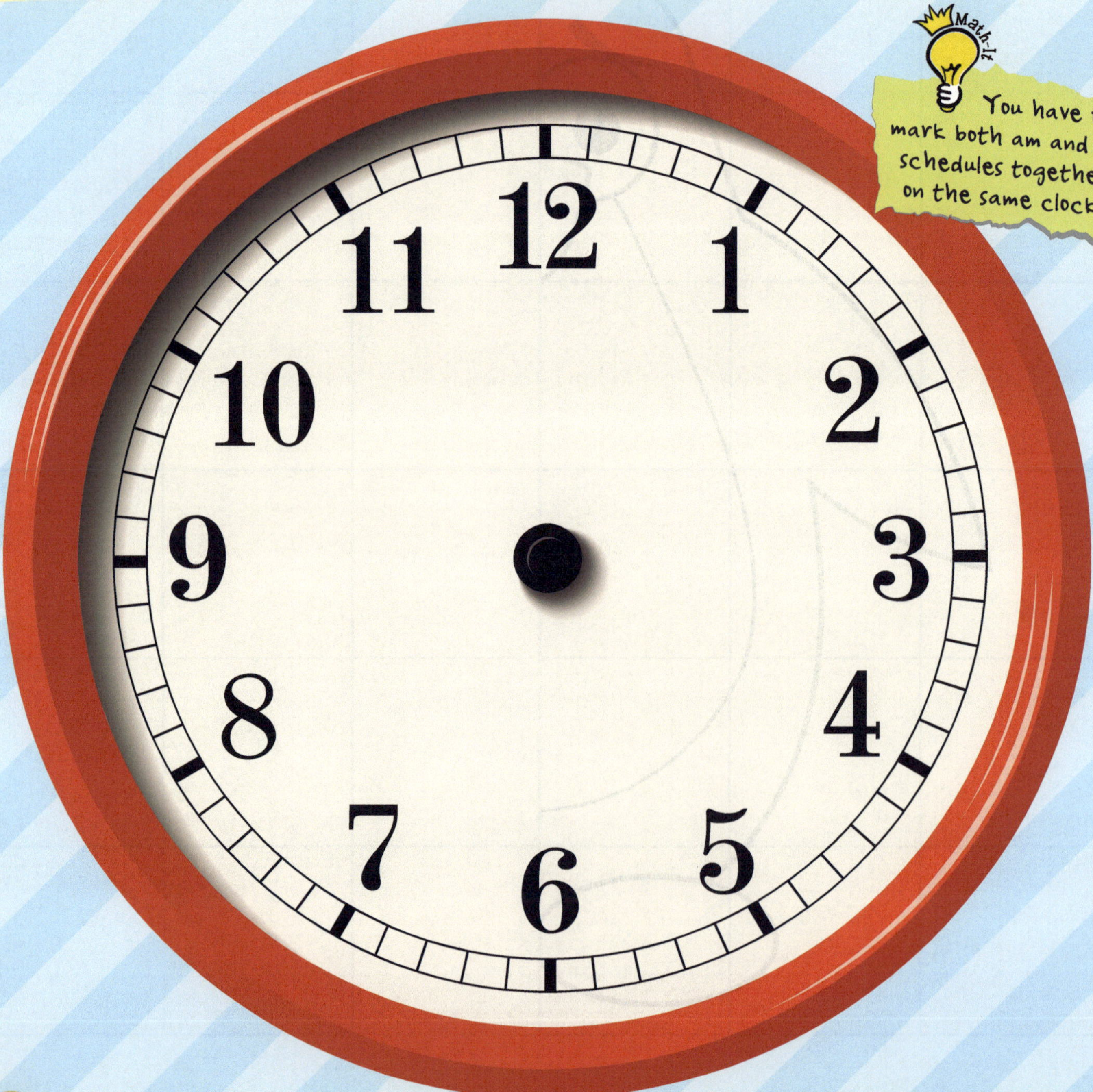

Special Calendar

Think of something special that happens in each month and draw it in the space provided. December has been done for you.

JANUARY	FEBRUARY	MARCH

APRIL	MAY	JUNE

JULY	AUGUST	SEPTEMBER

OCTOBER	NOVEMBER	DECEMBER

Ruler Rules

Look at the images on the ruler and write the length of each in the space provided. Colour the images that are more than 5 cm.

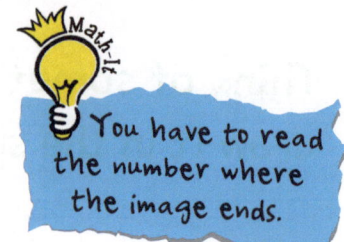

Math-It
You have to read the number where the image ends.

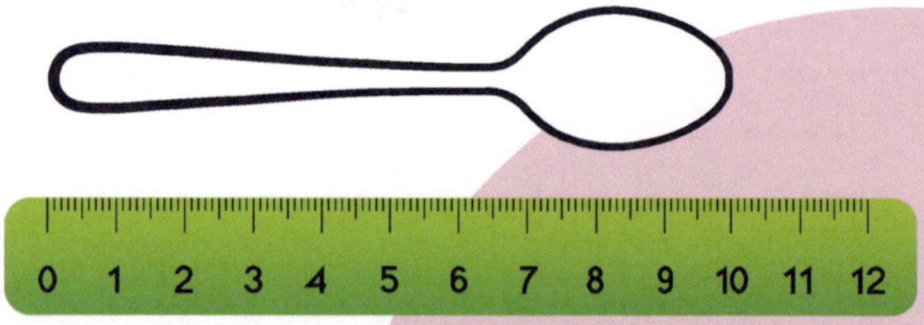
0 1 2 3 4 5 6 7 8 9 10 11 12

______ cm

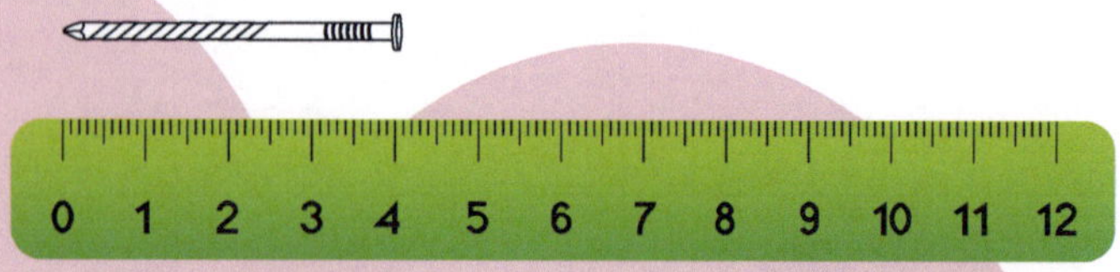
0 1 2 3 4 5 6 7 8 9 10 11 12

______ cm

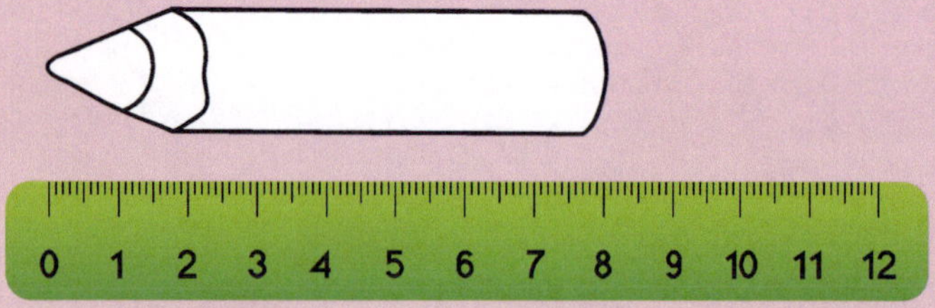
0 1 2 3 4 5 6 7 8 9 10 11 12

______ cm

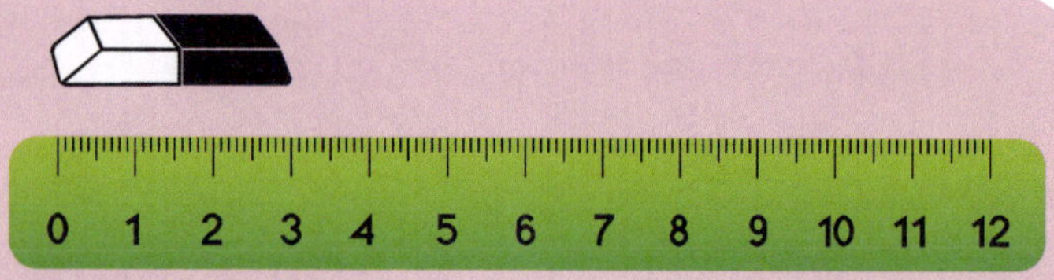
0 1 2 3 4 5 6 7 8 9 10 11 12

______ cm

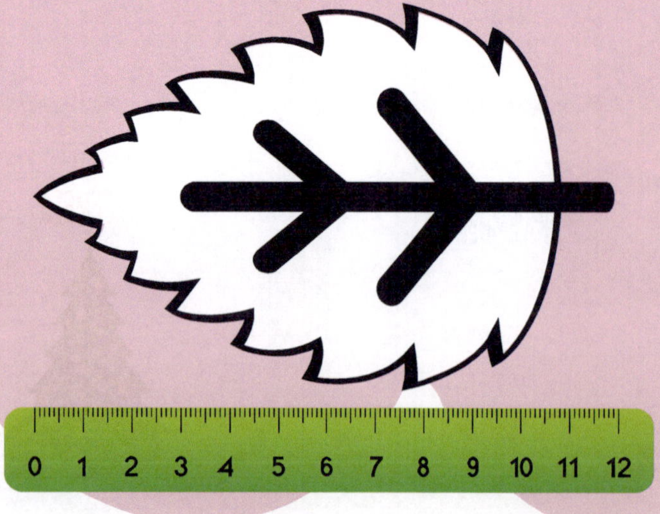
0 1 2 3 4 5 6 7 8 9 10 11 12

______ cm

Measuring Containers

Colour the container you would use to measure the following liquids.

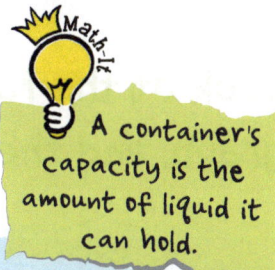

A container's capacity is the amount of liquid it can hold.

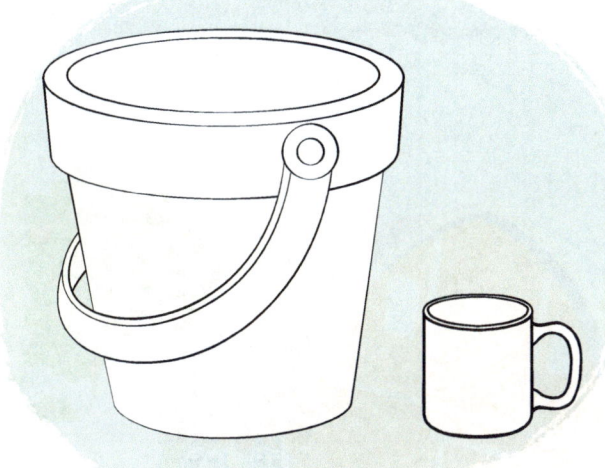

Milk you drink

Cough syrup

Water needed to wash some clothes

Juice you drink

At the Farm

Look at the farm below. Colour the animals that are asked on the graph, and then count and mark them.

Tally Art

Look at the objects below, and verify them against the tally marks mentioned. Only colour the objects where the tally marks DO NOT match the actual answer.

Ice-Cream Survey

Ask ten people their favourite flavour of ice cream and mark it on the cones below.

You can draw one scoop for each person.

Vanilla · Chocolate · Strawberry

Work Backwards

You can't use more or less shapes than mentioned already.

Make a design in the space provided using the shapes mentioned in the graph and then colour them.

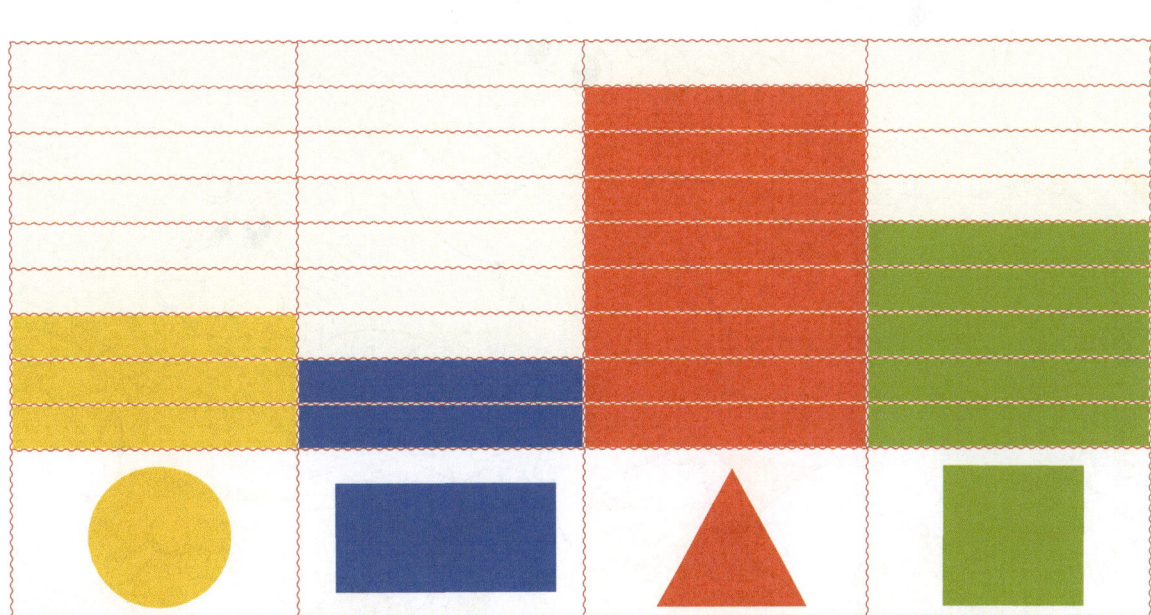

Running Wild

Answer the following questions by colouring the animals.

Colour the last animal brown
Colour the third animal black
Colour the first animal grey

Colour the second animal orange
Colour the fourth animal pink

Named

Use the blocks below to write and colour your name.

Avoid using part blocks to make the counting easier.

I used _____ number of blocks for my name.

Letter _____ needed the least blocks in my name.

Letter _____ needed the most blocks in my name.

Math-o-Bot's Challenge

A Fibonacci pattern is created by adding the previous two numbers to get the following number. Complete this pattern and also colour the squares based on the answers you get.

Here is the pattern: 1, 1, 2, 3, 5. The pattern is anti-clockwise.

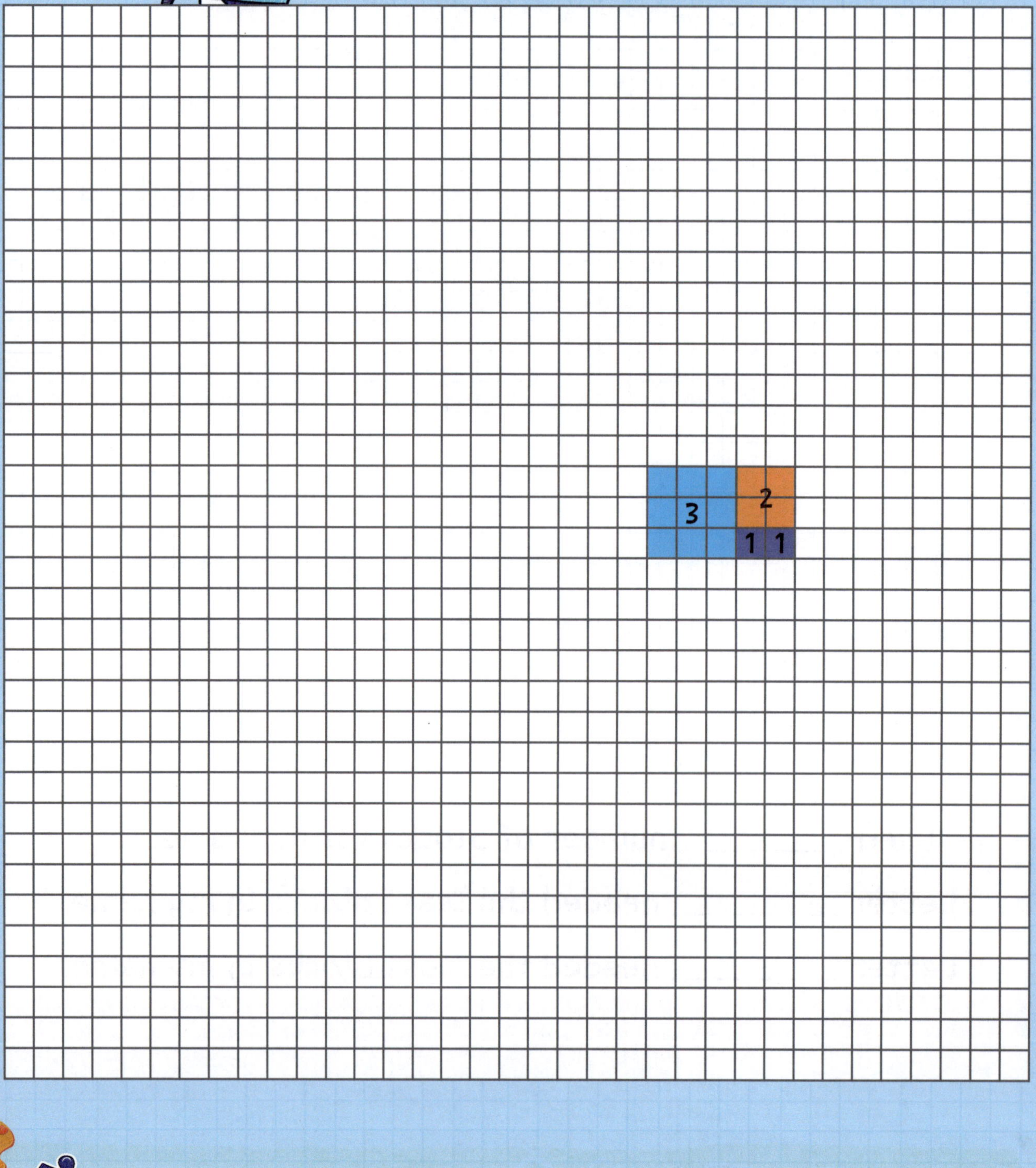

		2
3		
	1	1

Answers

Page 3

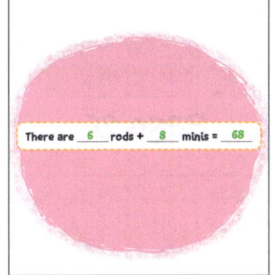

Page 4

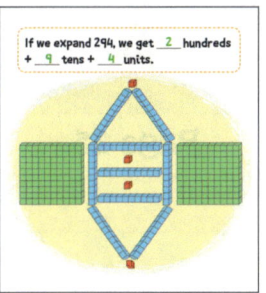

Page 5

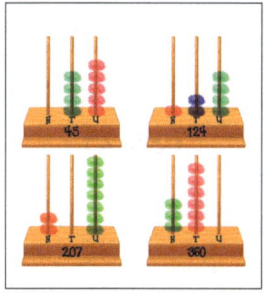

Page 6

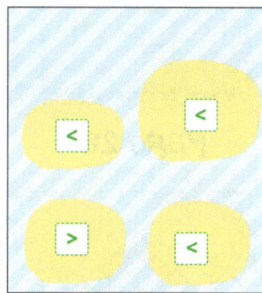

Page 7

Page 8

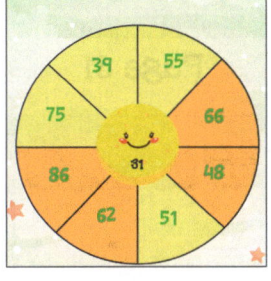

Page 9

Page 10

Page 11

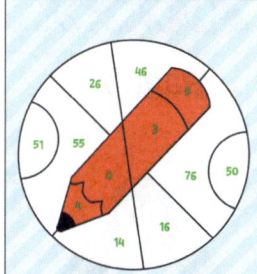

Page 12

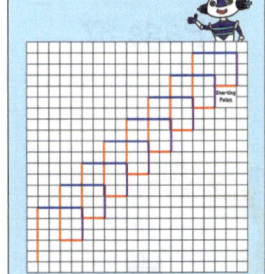

Page 13

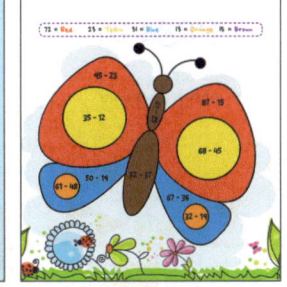

Page 14

Page 15

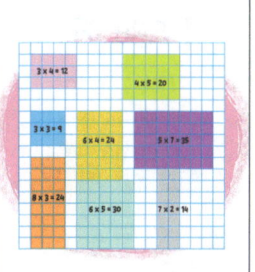

Page 16

Page 17

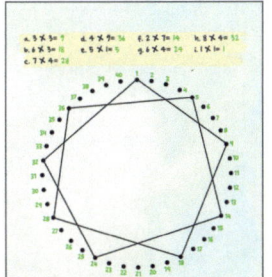
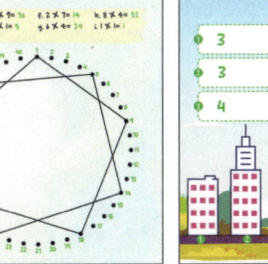

Page 18

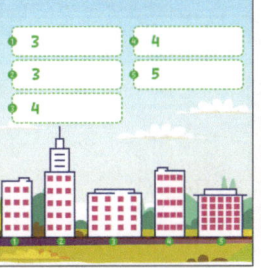

Page 19

Page 20

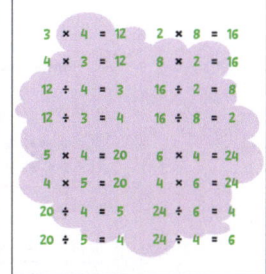

Page 21

Page 22

Page 23

Page 24

Page 25

Page 26

Page 27

Page 28

Page 29

Page 30

Page 31

Page 32

Page 33

Page 34

Page 35

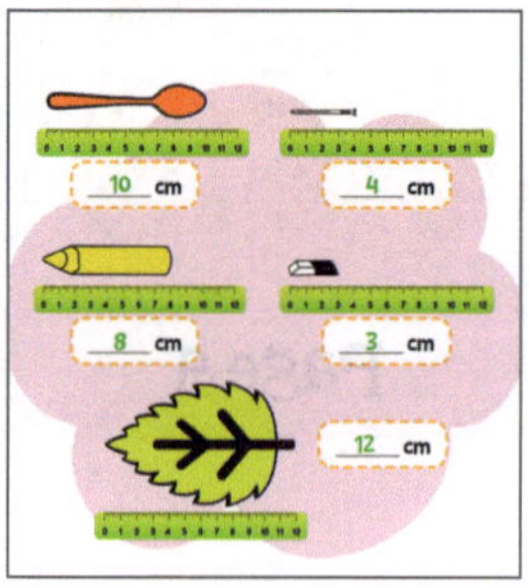

Page 36

Page 37

Page 38

Page 39

Page 40

Page 41

Page 42

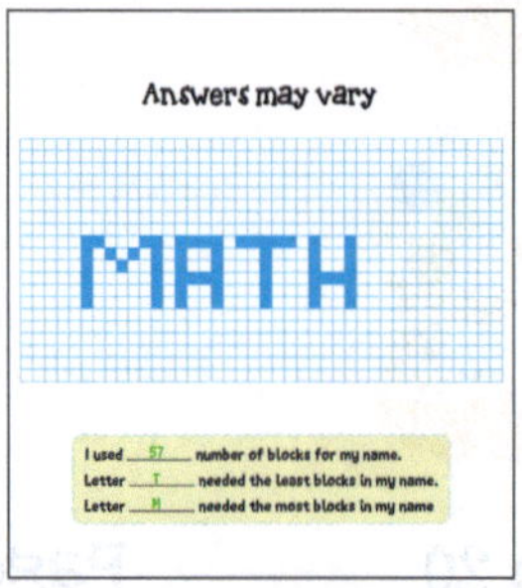

Page 43

Page 44